BROADENING THE CONSTITUTION

by

Kenneth Michael Weber

Library of Congress Control Number (LCCN): 9781966647805

ISBNs:
eBook: 978-1-966647-79-9
Paperback: 978-1-966647-80-5

Published by:
Authors Publishing House
178 Broadway, 3rd Floor, #1343
New York, NY 10001, USA

Main Line: (855) 624-0155
Email: support@authorspublishinghouse.com

NOTE FROM AUTHOR

I originally chose to write this anonymously because often, when our ideologies or sexual inclinations are challenged, we tend to seek to discredit the person rather than address the reason why we feel offended by the information. I would rather have everyone who reads this focus on whether what is said is true rather than who wrote it.

TABLE OF CONTENTS

ABORTION: A CONSTITUTIONAL RIGHT?

Rhetoric is the art of persuasion through effective speaking or writing. It studies the techniques used to inform, persuade, and motivate audiences. Rhetoric can involve language that may not be honest or reasonable.

I

PROCREATION: BIBLICAL UNDERSTANDING

To gain a perspective on abortion from a biblical perspective, one must understand creation and procreation.

God created a body from the dust of the earth and then breathed the breath of life into that body. At the entrance of the breath of life, man became a living soul. A soul is a spirit being with a mind, will, and emotions. It is vital to recognize that God breathed His life into man, which made mankind in the image and likeness of God. After the creation of Eve, He commanded them to be fruitful and multiply. In essence, He instructed them to bring forth others like themselves. In order for them to accomplish this, He gave them the two ingredients necessary: a body and the breath of life (His life).

The body begins as a cell placed in the womb of the woman, which we call an egg. God put the breath of life into a microscopic cell in the loins of the man, which we refer to as sperm. When observed under a microscope, sperm appear as moving particles, often referred to as swimmers. These particles would not move if there weren't any life in them. God then gave humanity a process based on their anatomical composition, whereby the breath of life could be breathed into the body. As it was when He created them, at the entrance of the breath of life, man becomes a living soul.

Contrary to the rhetoric of the American Medical Association, there are no trimesters in the development of life in the womb, but rather the development and the growth of the body in which the life that already exists will dwell. Anything done to that body that ends the process of this development is the taking of a life, whether inside or outside the womb. Though man can destroy the body, the soul still exists because it contains the spirit of life which comes from God; therefore, it is incapable of experiencing an end because God's life is eternal, and so also is the life in every soul into which his spirit enters. There is eternal existence for everyone and eternal life for those who embrace Jesus Christ as Lord and Savior.

Scripture further affirms this truth in the story of Sarah. When the angelic visitors came unto Abraham in his old age and told him that he would father a son by Sarah, her reaction brings perspective to the fact that women desire the pleasure of sex equally as men. Genesis 18 records the encounter:

> 9 They said to him, Where is Sarah thy wife? And he said, Behold, in the tent.
>
> 10 And he said, "I will certainly return unto thee according to the time of life; and, lo, Sarah thy wife shall have a son. And Sarah heard it in the tent door, which was behind him.
>
> 11 Now Abraham and Sarah were old and well stricken in age, and it ceased to be with Sarah after the manner of women. Therefore, Sarah laughed within herself, saying, "After I am waxed old, shall I have pleasure, my lord being old also?

13 And the Lord said unto Abraham, Wherefore did Sarah laugh, saying, Shall I of a surety bear a child, which am old?

When Sarah laughed, she was referencing and looking forward to the pleasure, the benefit of the process for which their bodies were restored. It was the angel, however, who focused upon the purpose of the process of creating and bearing a child. Nothing has changed from then until now. Mankind continues to focus on the benefits of the process; God focuses on the purpose. With the legalization of abortion, we have made pleasure the purpose of the reproductive process and God's purpose of procreation a matter of choice. This has led us to become servants to sexual pleasure.

The purpose of the reproductive process is further revealed in Scripture by Jesus in a conversation with the Sadducees in Matthew 22:

The purpose of the reproductive process is further revealed to us in scripture by Jesus in a conversation with the Sadducees in Matthew 22:

23 The same day came to him the Sadducees, which say that there is no resurrection, and asked him,

24 Saying, Master, Moses said, if a man dies, having no children, his brother shall marry his wife, and raise up seed unto his brother.

25 Now there were with us seven brethren: and the first, when he had married a wife, deceased, and, having no issue, left his wife unto his brother:

[26] Likewise, the second also, and the third, unto the seventh.

[27] And last of all, the woman died also.

[28] Therefore, in the resurrection, whose wife shall she be of the seven? For they all had her.

[29] Jesus answered and said unto them, Ye do err, not knowing the scriptures, nor the power of God.

[30] For in the resurrection they neither marry, nor are given in marriage, but are as the angels of God in heaven.

If there is no marriage, there is no sex in the kingdom of Heaven. This is not because God is against the pleasure of sex but because there is no longer any purpose for the reproductive process. Angels don't have sex because they don't reproduce themselves.

While studying and researching the subject of abortion, I came to this understanding. I then felt compelled to bring this truth to the attention of our leaders. Yet, the Holy Spirit immediately spoke, saying that they already knew it. This realization led me to wrestle with the question: if they already know, why then did our nation's leaders legalize abortion? And how is it rationalized and justified in their minds?

2

THE PURPOSE/THE ROOT CAUSE

10 "And now also the axe is laid unto the root of the trees." (Matthew 3:10)

Through prayer and research, I realized that abortion was not legalized for the express purpose of killing babies; rather, it was legalized for another purpose—one that, in the minds of those who supported it, outweighed the value of the unborn child's life and right to live.

To understand the purpose for which the whole of society seems to want to avoid acknowledging when addressing this issue, we must return to the time when abortion was legalized and look at the political and social climate then. It was a time of great turmoil in the nation, marked by the war in Vietnam, which many Americans protested, the Civil Rights movement, and women's efforts to gain equal rights in the political arena. In the social arena, young people were being expressive and rebelling against the social norms of our society. Everything was challenged, including our clothing, music, religious beliefs, and sexual expression.

During this time, there was a music festival which marked a turning point in our society, known as Woodstock. It attracted thousands of young people and lasted three days, during which it is alleged that there was drug use, public nudity, and sex. After this music fest, there were many young people who became what was known as Hippies; they believed and practiced what was known as free love, sex without commitment. Some began to live in communes where they felt free to practice living with this newfound freedom. This was the continuation of an activity said to have originated in the previous generation in American suburbs, known as wife swapping, where couples would gather at key parties and exchange spouses for a night. The effects of this can still be seen in our modern-day sexual revolution.

However, there was a major issue in the free love movement for young women. While men were free to be sexual with as many women as they desired, women had to be concerned with the possibility of conception. Thus, we unveil the root cause for which the right to end a pregnancy was fought for: to allow a female to be as free as a man in their desire to have sex without having to face the consequence of conception.

Understanding this fact allows us to see that abortion was and is legalized not for the express purpose of killing babies but rather to allow the woman the right to express herself as freely as a man and to decide whether she purposed to conceive during this act or whether it was just for pleasure. This fact negates the idea that it is the male factor that yearns after sex and the saying that refers to them as dogs.

Scripture speaks directly to this distortion of purpose. In 2 Timothy 3, Paul confirms that such a time would come:

> 1 This know also, that in the last days perilous times shall come.

> 2 For men shall be lovers of their own selves, covetous, boasters, proud, blasphemers, disobedient to parents, unthankful, unholy,
>
> 3 Without natural affection, trucebreakers, false accusers, incontinent (lacking self-control), fierce, despisers of those that are good,
>
> 4 Traitors, heady, high-minded, lovers of pleasures more than lovers of God.
>
> 5 Having a form of godliness, but denying the power thereof:

The fact that the pursuit of pleasure was the reason for the legalization of abortion raises the question of whether the freedom to express oneself freely sexually without responsibility is a constitutional right. The legalization of abortion by the Supreme Court suggests that they determined it was. However, the justices who voted in favor of this right did not explicitly state that it was included in the Constitution. Instead, they argued that the Constitution was broad enough to include this right.

This raises another question of constitutionality: whether the constitution can be discriminatory in granting this freedom based on gender. The male, or father of the child, who contributes equally to the formation of the child, has no rights over the life of that child. The woman alone decides whether the child lives or dies. At the same time, the government that granted her the right to act sexually irresponsible also holds the male financially responsible if she decides to keep the child. In the spirit of equality under the

Constitution, does he not have the right to decide whether he was engaging in a reproductive act or an act solely for pleasure?

The male and father is reduced to the equivalent of a sperm-emitting dildo with no mind, thoughts, heart, and absolutely no rights over the life of his seed, according to the government. Isn't it discriminatory for the government to hold him financially responsible if the woman decides to keep the child against his will? He shares no right in deciding the fate of his child; he has no right to determine the purpose of entering into the sexual relationship, as the woman does, and yet he is held responsible by the government against his will for the financial support of the child. While the reason for this discriminatory act is evident, it is likely that the U.S. government may ultimately have to provide welfare for the child if the mother is financially unable to do so. Yet this does not change the fact that such enforcement does not align with constitutional principles. Further, since the government legalized the right to be sexually irresponsible to woman, it is no more than right that the government share in the consequences and responsibility of their decision.

3

THE RHETORIC AND THE CONSEQUENCE

Since abortion was legalized, there has been a battle between those who support it and those who are against it. Throughout this battle, there have been quotes or sayings that reveal one's stance on the issue. Understanding the meaning of rhetoric and its role as the basis of American politics is important. Rhetoric, though it may be convincing, does not have to be factual or accurate. Even Christian leaders have embraced the subject of abortion from a rhetorical perspective, declaring their political perspective as the truth of God.

Let's look at these sayings from a perspective of truth. If we are to seek the truth, we must consider how God views the subject and what His Word says. Concerning children, Scripture declares in Psalm 127:3, "Lo, children are a heritage of the Lord: and the fruit of the womb is his reward." God views children as his valued and personal reward from mankind. The first thing he told Adam and Eve was to be fruitful and multiply and to replenish (constantly fill) the earth.

When we look at the man's choice to be either pro-choice or pro-life from a biblical perspective, it turns out to lack truth because it is God who gives us life, and it is God who gives man the right to choose. He placed the tree of life and the tree of the knowledge of good and evil in the garden and instructed humanity not to eat from the tree of the knowledge of good and evil; this involves the freedom to choose. What is important to note here is that He also informed them of the consequences for making the wrong choice. Consequence is something that seems to be far removed from our society. Sadly, even in the church, where it is said that God is a good God and has nothing to do with the tragedies that befall mankind, no matter how far we stray from His purpose and plans for our lives. It totally confuses me when I hear a minister say that God is the God of Abraham, Isaac, and Jacob, the God of Israel, but He is no longer the God of judgment. Even though the prophets spoke of the judgment of God, and He says of Himself that He is the same yesterday, today, and tomorrow, He does not change.

Therefore, when the leaders of the Supreme Court establish laws that violate or change the laws of God in our nation, it does not eliminate the consequences of those deeds in God's sight, which he spoke concerning such deeds or activities. God spoke unto Israel and warned them against the shedding of innocent blood in Deuteronomy 19:10, "That innocent blood be not shed in thy land, which the Lord thy God giveth thee for an inheritance, and so blood be upon thee." There is no greater innocent and vulnerable state of human existence than in the womb of the mother.

Although we refuse to acknowledge the consequences of legalized abortion, we are living them every day. Few are willing to point it out, even though it is clearly seen. Legalizing abortion took the most absolute fact of the right to life and made it subjective. We now live in a society where the value of life is no longer absolute, but somewhat subjective, even among our young people. One of the major sayings of adults today when referring to this generation is, "I don't know what is wrong with the children of today; they have no value for life, their own, or others." The Supreme Court of many states has declared that human life has no absolute value, but rather the value of a child's life is subject to the mother's will.

Consequently, there seems to be very little that remains absolute. Sexual expression involves no absolute either in means of expression or in the choice of partners. Even at birth, there is no absolute value placed upon the genitalia of a child for determining gender; this, too, is subjective despite clear evidence thereof.

Intercourse between husband and wife was purposed for reproduction. The consequences of prioritizing pleasure are evident, as there is no limit to how far we will go in seeking gratification. There is no longer any restraining measure of morality. Naturally or orally, vaginally or anally, privately or publicly, consensually or by force, with the opposite sex or the same sex, one of no kin or next of kin, child or aged, mankind or animal, fruit, plastic or rubber, pleasing oneself or being pleased by another doesn't matter when a society becomes a servant to pleasure.

The binding and infliction of pain, which is criminal under natural law, is sought after, even paid for, in the pursuit of pleasure. We have reached a place where we no longer know how to build true relationships or friendships without it involving sex. Intimacy in the marital relationship was once considered sacred and the violation of this bond considered adultery by either party, but now there is a growing acceptance of the idea that there is no longer an absolute value to the commitment of one's body to their mate only; this is also subjective.

The bond of marriage has evolved with the emergence of open relationships, threesomes, and polyamory, which suggest that it is possible to love and be intimate with more than one person. In addition, swinging, a more modern term for orgies, involves partners alternating between different people in a sort of sexual playground. Unlike polyamory, those who engage in swinging do not involve emotions; they emphasize that their interactions are purely sexual. There are also individuals who do not participate in these activities themselves but find enjoyment in observing others through technology. This brings to mind the words of God, which state: "Who knowing the judgment of God, that they which commit such things are worthy of death, not only do the same, but have pleasure in them that do them."

Again, nothing has an absolute value; everything is subjective. A more confusing form of things being subjective is the fact that a woman can have actual intercourse in the process of making a movie for which she is paid for all the world to see, and she is called a movie star. Another woman may have sex in a porn video for which she is paid, and she is called a porn star. Neither is prosecuted for violating any law. Yet another woman who has sex in private, for which she is paid is called a prostitute, has broken some law of morality. Is the moral law that she has broken based upon the fact that the public does not get to enjoy viewing the prostitute in her profession, or that she does not have a legal way of reporting her earnings, which would make economics the foundation of our morality as a nation? Again, there is no absolute; it is subjective. Maybe a prostitute should call herself a "prostistar" or film her activities and publish them, and that would free her of violating any law.

As it was in the garden, so it is now. We have been given the freedom to choose, but the consequence of a wrong choice violates our relationship with God and with each other and is destructive. Remember Eve yielded because that which was forbidden was presented by the serpent in a manner which was pleasing to her sight (lust of the eyes), good for food (lust of the flesh), to make her equal to God (pride of life)—the three things by which marriages, families, relationships, and societies are destroyed.

In acknowledging that we have reached a point where there is no absolute standard or code of behavior, one must look back to the calculated erosion of the personage and standard that represented an absolute code of ethics and morals: God and His Word. Consider the following examples:

a) Separation of church and state
b) Prayer out of schools
c) Prayer at school graduations and sports events banned
d) Bibles out of school
e) Ten Commandments banned from school.
f) Ten Commandments banned in government facilities
g) Ministers are not allowed to pray at public events

The list goes on, but what we can plainly see is that those who supported a secular form of government knew that to promote this mentality, they had to remove the standard of the absolute truth of God and Jesus Christ and anything that represented the acknowledgment of His existence or communication with Him. Thus, we find ourselves in our present state, lacking a moral standard and fighting for the right for everyone to do what is right in their own eyes.

4

JURY DUTY

Many years ago, there was a city where the citizens purchased the greater percentage of their food from three farmers on the outskirts of town. The farmers were Mr. A, Mr. B, and Mr. C. One year, a storm came through and destroyed the farms of the only nearby farmers from whom the people of the city could buy. Seeing that the people had no alternative but to pay whatever price they were offered for their crops, and that people from nearby towns would also need their produce, Mr. A decided they would raise their prices to take advantage of the situation.

Mr. A realized that he needed the cooperation of the other farmers to avoid appearing unfair or greedy. Therefore, he approached Mr. B to share his idea. Mr. B agreed, but only because he thought Mr. C would be on board, which he doubted would happen. Next, Mr. A met with Mr. C to present his thoughts and plans. Mr. C responded by reminding Mr. A that for years they had prospered, built their homes, and raised their children with the support of the community. He expressed concern about taking advantage of the people now, especially since they felt they had no other choice but to pay the higher prices.

Mr. A reported back to Mr. B with Mr. C's response, which came as no surprise. Mr. A told him not to worry, he would take care of it, but did not reveal his plan. Knowing that there was a controlled product that a farmer could buy to put in his farm's irrigation system, which would kill the seed but not harm the soil for future planting, he purchased a bottle. Late one night, after they had all planted their crops, he added it to Mr. C's irrigation system.

As time went by, the crops of the other farmers began to bud, but Mr. C saw that his crops were not budding, so he became concerned. He gave it some more time, and when there was still no growth, he began to dig up his seed to see what could possibly have gone wrong, but was unable to find anything except that the seeds seemed to have rotted. He thought perhaps he had bought bad seed.

Mr. C's daughter was engaged to Mr. B's son, and on the night that Mr. A put the chemicals in his irrigation system, he saw his truck parked by his fiancée's farm but thought nothing of it due to the relationship these farmers had with one another. Hearing the news of what was happening, he mentioned to Mr. C. that he had observed Mr. A's truck parked on the edge of his farmland late one night after dropping his daughter off from a date. Not wanting to believe that his lifelong friend would do anything to hurt him, yet considering the conversation he had with him, he decided he needed to look into it further before falsely accusing his friend. He therefore dug up some of the soil containing the rotted seed and brought it to be tested, and it was determined that the seed contained a very harmful chemical. Still not wanting to confront Mr. A without any evidence, he sought the help of a lawyer, who hired an investigator.

The investigator checked the closest place where this product could be purchased but found no record of Mr. A purchasing this controlled substance. Not convinced, he went to the store of a neighboring state and found that there was a record of Mr. A purchasing two bottles of this controlled substance. Armed with this information, charges were filed against him, and in a subsequent surprise search of his home, the second bottle of the substance was discovered.

In a lawsuit for punitive damages after being found guilty, Mr. A's lawyer argued that his client was only responsible for repaying the price of the seed since there was no development of the plants. Mr. C's lawyer argued that he was responsible for the value of his crop because of the potential of the life of the seed. You are a juror serving on this case. How do you judge? Is he responsible just for the seed or for the price of the crop that the seed would have yielded?

The moral and purpose of the story is to provoke thought regarding a matter of much greater significance. When the Righteous Judge comes to judge the deeds of man, will he count the lives of the over 65 million babies who were aborted as a seed that was destroyed, or will he hold those responsible for the person they were in the womb and destined to be outside of the womb?

NOTHING WRITTEN IS EVER INTENDED FOR CONDEMNATION BUT RATHER REALIZATION—THAT WE MIGHT REALIZE HOW GOD VIEWS OUR ACTIONS, REPENT, AND BE FORGIVEN THROUGH FAITH IN JESUS CHRIST

5

WOMEN'S RIGHTS

Having children was once something that women sought after, but now, we have a childless movement. There is no shame to a woman who does not have children; however, to celebrate and promote being childless will diminish future societies and make them unable to function fully. The most valuable resource on earth is people. It is people who place the value on everything else, not the opposite.

The Bible accurately states that in the last days, men shall become lovers of pleasure more than lovers of God. There is no absolute. Thirteen states now view the preborn as children, which entitles them to human rights. The states that recognize this simple fact are as follows: Alabama, Arkansas, Idaho, Illinois, Kansas, Kentucky, Mississippi, Oklahoma, Tennessee, Texas, Louisiana, Missouri, and Michigan.

> 18 U.S. Code § 1841 - Protection of unborn children
> - U.S. Code
> - Notes
>
> **(a)**
>
> (1)
>
> Whoever engages in conduct that violates any of the provisions of law listed in subsection (b) and thereby causes the death of, or bodily injury (as defined in section 1365) to, a child, who is in

utero at the time the conduct takes place, is guilty of a separate offense under this section.

(2)

(A) Except as otherwise provided in this paragraph, the punishment for that separate offense is the same as the punishment provided under Federal law for that conduct had that injury or death occurred to the unborn child's mother.

(B) An offense under this section does not require proof that—

(i) the person engaging in the conduct had knowledge or should have had knowledge that the victim of the underlying offense was pregnant; or

(ii) the defendant intended to cause the death of, or bodily injury to, the unborn child.

(C) If the person engaging in the conduct thereby intentionally kills or attempts to kill the unborn child, that person shall, instead of being punished under subparagraph (A), be punished as provided under sections 1111, 1112, and 1113 of this title for intentionally killing or attempting to kill a human being.

(D) Notwithstanding any other provision of law, the death penalty shall not be imposed for an offense under this section.

(b)

The provisions referred to in subsection (a) are the following:

(1)

(c)

> Nothing in this section shall be construed to permit prosecution.
>
> (1)
>
> of any person for conduct relating to an abortion for which the consent of the pregnant woman, or a person authorized by law to act on her behalf, has been obtained or for which such consent is implied by law.
>
> (2)
> of any person for any medical treatment of the pregnant woman or her unborn child; or
>
> (3)
> of any woman with respect to her unborn child.
>
> **(d)**
>
> As used in this section, the term "unborn child" means a child in utero, and the term "child in utero" or "child, who is in utero" means a member of the species homo sapiens, at any stage of development, who is carried in the womb.
>
> (Added Pub. L. 108–212, § 2(a), Apr. 1, 2004, 118 Stat. 568; Cornell Law School)

I displayed the above law to help us understand how confused we have become as a nation about what is right or wrong. Under one section of the law, a person can be charged with the wrongful death of a child in the uterus if an act of violence is committed, which resulted in the death of the child, except if it is due to a medical process or by consent of the mother of the child. The medical process to save the life of the mother may warrant subjection to the will of the mother but has become a means of justification for the taking of the life of a child where there is no threat of harm to the mother.

The most absurd and inhumane portion of this law is where it states that there is no prosecution if the mother consents to an abortion. Therefore, it is safe to conclude that what is considered a violent act is no longer considered to be violent when a woman consents to it. To stick a needle into the head of a child in the womb to cause its death is not a violent act. To cut a baby apart limb by limb while in the womb is not a violent act when the mother of the child consents to it. In what realm of reason does this have any resemblance to a society governed by truth or justice when that society, in essence, states that: A WOMAN IS ABOVE THE LAW.

We have confirmed that the freedom to be sexually irresponsible is not guaranteed by any constitutional right; however, it is a matter of personal choice. Ending the life of a child does not fall under personal choice. Once a child is conceived, the personal choice of whether to engage in sexual intercourse or with whom one chooses transitions into personal responsibility, which is shared equally by both the mother and father of the child conceived.

In the beginning, in the garden, Satan deceived Eve and told her she could be like God. Now in these last days, politicians have made her like God, having the power of life and death.

6

MY BODY, MY CHOICE

In the recent presidential election, this phrase was used to express a woman's right to control her reproductive process. I don't think that women realize the full spiritual impact of this statement. To understand why I say this, we must realize that the sperm of a man not only contains the DNA of the man but also the breath of life that comes from God. It is the breath of life that creates another life; therefore, it is safe to conclude that the reproductive process involves God, man, and the woman.

We know that the government has reduced the male to a sperm emitting dildo with no mind, heart or rights concerning the unborn child, his humanity is acknowledged in financial responsibility if the woman chooses to have the child by our government With this statement she is saying even though It is God that gives life it is the woman who decides whether the child lives or dies. She says this even though God has stated that children are valued possessions to Him and the fruit of the womb is His reward. In the beginning, the woman was deceived into believing that she could be equal to God, but in these days, she has been deceived into believing that she is equal to God, with power over life and death unless she agrees otherwise. Those who understand scripture know that God, in His longsuffering nature, allows man time to reconsider his actions and to repent before He establishes the fact that "the earth is the

Lord's and the fullness thereof, the world and they that dwell therein."

The longsuffering of God and His mercy are clearly seen in Scripture. When God promised Abraham that his descendants would inherit the land that He had shown him, He told him that it would be 400 years before they would enter into the land because the iniquity of the Amorites was not yet full. They would continue for another 400 years before judgment would come.

Another example of God's longsuffering is seen in His dealings with the nation of Israel when they began to embrace the teachings of the Gentiles on the god Baal. After many years, God sent his prophet to challenge 450 prophets of Baal and show the people of Israel that He is the only God.

I know that some say that these are only Bible stories, and what do they have to do with abortion? Let me tell you a story of how the mindset of women in America could totally change concerning abortion. There could come a time when God shuts up the womb of every woman in America, and she could enjoy the pleasure of a sexual relationship without any concern of conception, since pleasure is the purpose of the sexual relationship. Young wives would desire to start a family and would turn to their husbands, but they would say, "I can give you pleasure, but it is not within my power to give you a child." Mothers would ask their sons and daughters, "When will you make me a grandmother?" and they would reply, "We have much pleasure, but we cannot conceive seed." They would turn to alternative measures, but nothing would work.

After several years of childlessness, one woman would be seen pregnant, and many would ask how she had conceived when no one else could. She would answer that she went before the Lord in repentance and promised Him that if He allowed her to conceive, she would never again prevent conception. When news of this spread throughout the nation, repentance would follow, and an explosion in the birth rate would occur. Abortion would no longer be sought in America.

This story illustrates how quickly a people's values can shift when confronted with the reality of God's authority over life. Yet in our present time, rather than turning toward repentance, the phrase "My Body, My Choice" has expanded beyond personal declaration. What began as an individual slogan soon became a rallying cry in the public square, enshrined in political rhetoric. Abortion thus moved beyond personal choice and entered the realm of parties, courts, and campaigns, where truth was replaced by persuasion and the pursuit of power.

The politics of abortion has since been divided by whether one is Republican or Democrat, conservative or liberal. Much like the arguments about constitutionality, these divisions rest not on truth but on rhetoric. Political parties or individual politicians must appeal to the perspectives and views of the general public in some way to gain their vote. It is no different in terms of moral issues. Their political platforms or campaigning do not have to reflect their personal convictions; they just have to be what the voters want to hear or believe.

In my research on the history of abortion in America, I found this to be particularly true. First, they say that the Republican Party stands against abortion; however, if you go back to the decision of *Roe v. Wade*, you will find that the facts do not support the implication. There were more Republican-nominated Supreme Court justices than Democratic ones, and yet the final vote was 7 to 2. The Supreme Court justice who wrote the opinion against legalizing abortion was a Democratic-nominated justice, and the justice who wrote the opinion in favor of legalizing it was a Republican-nominated justice. This fact offers no support to the claim of the Republicans standing for God or morality, as claimed by church members, or to the fact that they are Conservative.

Only one Republican-nominated justice voted against legalizing abortion. In fact, if one were to research the Supreme Court decisions as I have, one would find that every decision, previously mentioned concerning prayer, the Bible, ministers, and the Ten Commandments, received the support of Republican-nominated justices. People may lie, but facts are simply that—facts. They are objective and do not come with an opinion.

As a Christian and a minister, I find it disturbing when I hear ministers and pastors promote their opinion in politics as the truth of God. It is not that they express their opinion to which they have a right, but rather that they present it as the word of God, especially because it has no foundation in truth or fact. If you listen to the rhetoric presented by them, you will think that Jesus was a Republican and required everyone who followed him to be one, too. PREPOSTEROUS! Jesus Christ and God's word is the standard of righteousness and not the Republican party or any other political party or person. Thus, the rhetoric that begins as personal slogans does not stop there; it extends into politics and even the church, shaping opinions under the guise of truth.

7

CHURCH RHETORIC

If political rhetoric has shaped how abortion is debated in the public square, church rhetoric has shaped how it is preached in the pulpit. Sadly, many believers have allowed political allegiance to blur the line between God's truth and partisan opinion. This confusion has led to slogans in the church that sound convincing but fail to align with the Word of God.

Republicans are on God's side.

During the fifty years of *Roe v. Wade*, 27 years were under a Republican president, and 23 under a Democrat, yet abortions prevailed. The abortion rate was higher when a Republican was president than when a Democrat served.

Liberals support having abortions, and not Conservatives.

There have been over 65 million abortions in the United States since 1973. If most of these were by liberals or Democrats, one would have to conclude that there would be a much higher percentage of conservative Republican voters than liberals, giving them a clear advantage in political races. That would negate the need to violate the nation's capital before the world because their candidate lost the election. When it comes to having abortions, the difference is liberals do it liberally and openly, while conservatives do it conservatively and privately, but they both do it.

When a righteous Republican rules, the people rejoice.

Roe v. Wade was legalized in 1973 under a Republican president and overturned 50 years later under a Democratic president. There were other Supreme Court decisions that denied the sovereignty of God made while we had Republican presidents. Rhetoric gets votes because it convinces people and tells them what they want to hear, but when it comes to the truth, it does not measure up, regardless of where it is spoken—in the political arena or in the church, by a politician or a man of God.

If a Christian votes for a Democrat, they are cursed.

This statement goes beyond rhetoric into outright deception. There is absolutely no truth to it. This statement implies that Republicans represent the righteousness of God. My reply to this implication is: Where were the Republicans when prayer was taken out of the schools, when bible reading was banned, abortions legalized, and prayer was banned from public sports events? Wasn't it a Republican-nominated Supreme Court justice who cast the deciding vote in favor of same sex marriage? Why haven't past and present Republican presidents sought to overturn the laws that have removed the voice and influence of God's word from the political arena? Have the leaders of the church lost their voice in government through the separation of church and state and settled for the Republicans being our voice in exchange for the Christian vote? In conclusion, a vote for a Republican is no different from a vote for a Democrat, and neither determines our relationship with God, which comes only through faith in Jesus Christ and righteous living.

One day, Jesus is sitting among all the children who had been aborted and teaching them about life on earth. During the course of the conversation, the subject of politics arises, and one of them raises his hand to speak. Jesus permits him. He says that he has read heaven's books on politics on earth and discovered that when he came to heaven, there was a Republican president who was pro-life and stood against abortion. He says this with the same sense of pride expressed by Christians and pro-life advocates on earth who are Republican.

Another sits among them and shakes his head after hearing what was said. Jesus, noticing his reaction, asks if he has something to say. He says that he has also read heaven's books on politics on earth and learned that, contrary to the other person, when he came to heaven, there was a Democratic president who was pro-choice and ran his campaign on the women's right to have abortions. He then turns to the other person who had spoken and asks, "How long did you spend on earth outside of your mother's womb?"

Realizing the wisdom of the question and the answer, he bows his head and answers, "None," to which his counterpart replies, "Neither did I." Jesus then responds to them both, saying, "Oh, that it were done on earth as it is in heaven."

FOOD FOR THOUGHT

How broad is the Constitution?

The question we must ask ourselves as a nation is whether the pursuit of sexual freedom is covered by the Constitution, even to the point of justifying the abortion of innocent babies. Since the Constitution has already been broadened to include same sex marriage, will it be found to be broad enough in the future to extend this freedom to all those who seek sexual fulfillment by other means? Will incest be covered by the right to the pursuit of sexual freedom, or pedophilia or bestiality for those who choose to express themselves in this manner? Will public nudity or public sex be a constitutional right?

I know that asking these questions may seem absurd to some, yet to others, it merely exposes the desires of their hearts. This is the result of a nation that has chosen to separate God from its government. Every man does that which is right in his own eyes.

Made in the USA
Monee, IL
04 November 2026

67378716R00022